SPECTROSCOPY

Original Music Composed and Arranged by

Jack Mitchell Smith

Cover Art by

Lucy Blackwell

Copyright © 2020 West Kingston Productions Ltd.
978-1-6780-7002-1

"What do I write about 2020 that hasn't already been said?....

Well - amid the chaos, it was a year in which many dreams were finally born, as people were all of a sudden finding the time to pursue their creative goals. This was certainly true of myself, having found myself finally able to focus on my music full time. But what to do? How to start? For what to aim?

Having played a little Debussy for my own entertainment (if we can assume that playing Debussy is, indeed, a pleasure), I was very intrigued by his 'throwing out the rulebook' approach to piano playing and composition. He didn't seem to follow any structure or conventional technique, and so I concluded - why should I? I could compose a short piece of music that seems both beautiful yet inexplicable. Bizarre. Somehow ominous.......

.....and that I did. This became 'Krishna' - once a throwaway composition, but one that would become the foundation of a brand new project.

Being a composer gives me unlimited freedom in creating my music. That is to say I don't need to feel typecast and so, once the peculiarities of 'Krishna' were out of my system, other very different pieces followed. I didn't initially consider putting them together into a suite of music until a few compositions in. This was especially true seeing as I was experimenting with a new instrument to lead each new composition. Fancy writing a whole suite of music where each instrumentalist only has a couple of minutes to shine in the whole thing! Nonetheless, I persisted until I had conquered another two short but sweet pieces (which would go on to become 'Father of the Fatherland' and 'Precious Gold').

The titles were to come later, however (as, indeed, was the title 'Krishna').

Along with many others, the rainbow was one of the symbols that was present in 2020. Perhaps subconsciously this was the inspiration for how it would all fit together, but it certainly began somewhere and evolved into the idea of using the colours of the spectrum as a journey. Once I had established this, finding the themes for the remaining compositions was even more fun!

Research into the remaining colours for which I hadn't already applied one of my existing three pieces proved exciting, interesting and somewhat sneaky. Almost like a game - see how well I can disguise the meaning of the colours in the titles. See if people recognise that indigo is the colour of our intuition, which has been poetically termed the 'whisper of the soul', or know the link between tyrian purple and the Spiny Dye-Murex. More cunningly still, hiding the colour green within Ireland's 'lucky clover' history - it's just like a three leaf clover, plus one extra leaf.......

Anyway, that's where my role as historian ends and musician must recommence, as I invite you now on a journey through the different textures and colours of the spectrum.

Enjoy.............."

Jack Mitchell Smith, 2021

SPECTROSCOPY

'Kimono'

Page 1

'Father of the Fatherland'

Page 7

'Precious Gold'

Page 10

'Three Plus One'

Page 16

'Krishna'

Page 19

'Whisper of the Soul'

Page 22

'Murex Shell'

Page 26

Kimono

'Spectroscopy' - Part One

Jack Mitchell Smith

Father of the Fatherland

'Spectroscopy' - Part Two

Jack Mitchell Smith

Precious Gold

'Spectroscopy' - Part Three

Jack Mitchell Smith

62
p
8va
65
67
mp
8va
mp
69
mp

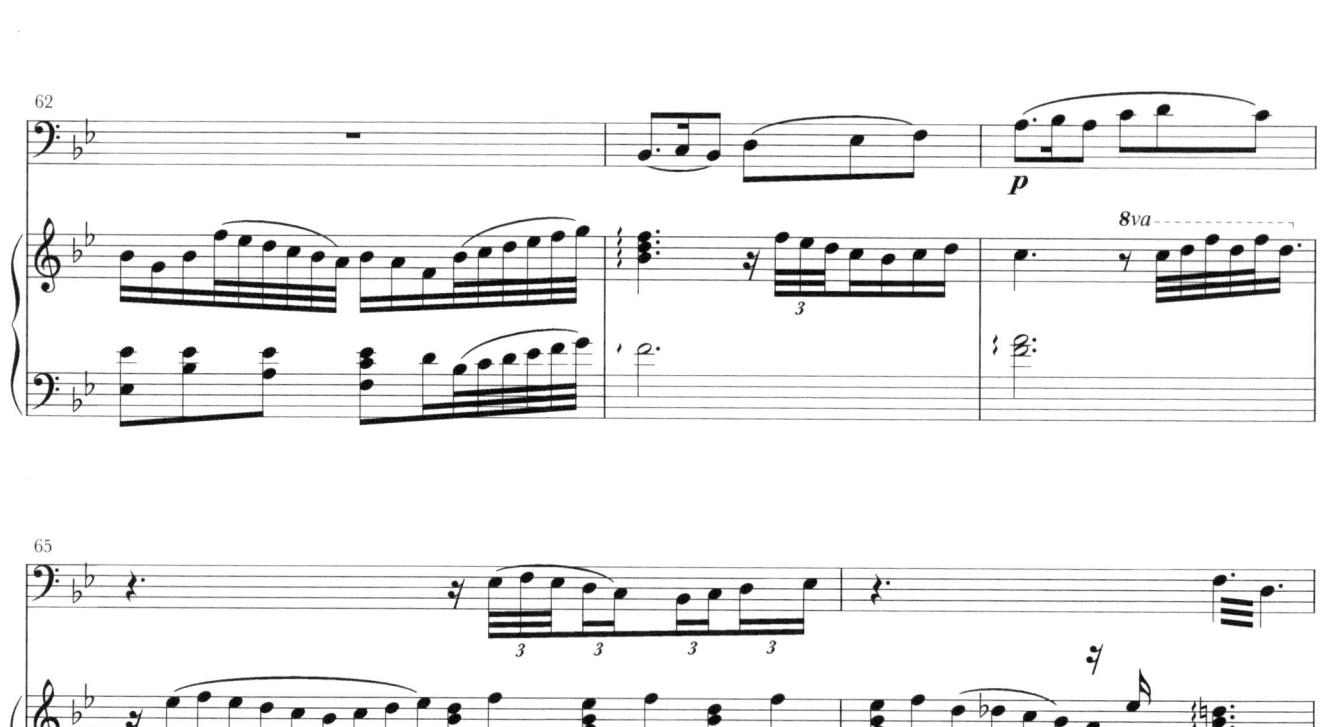

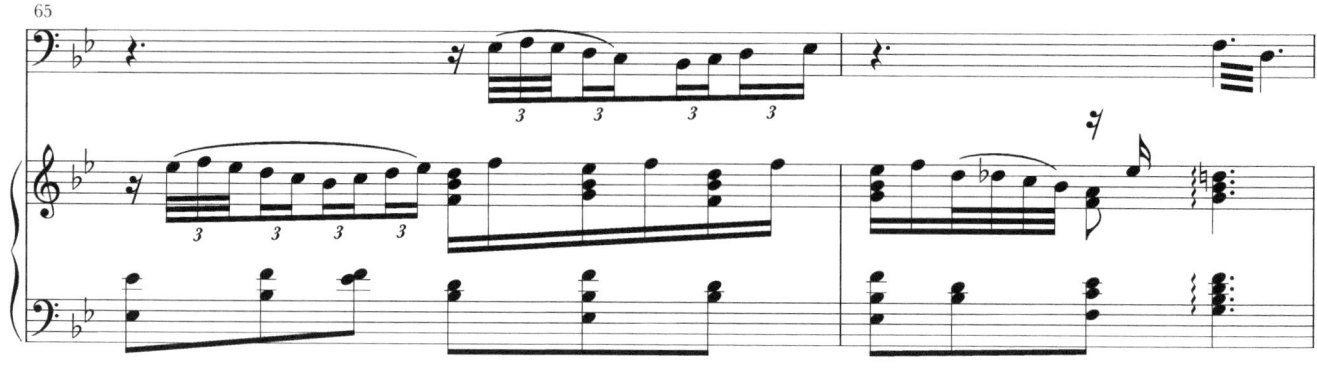

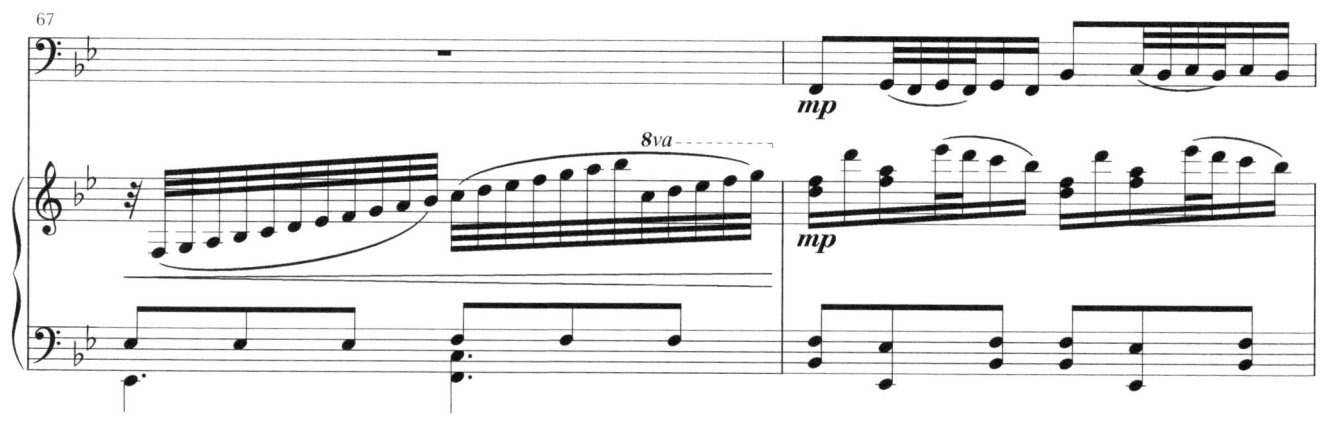

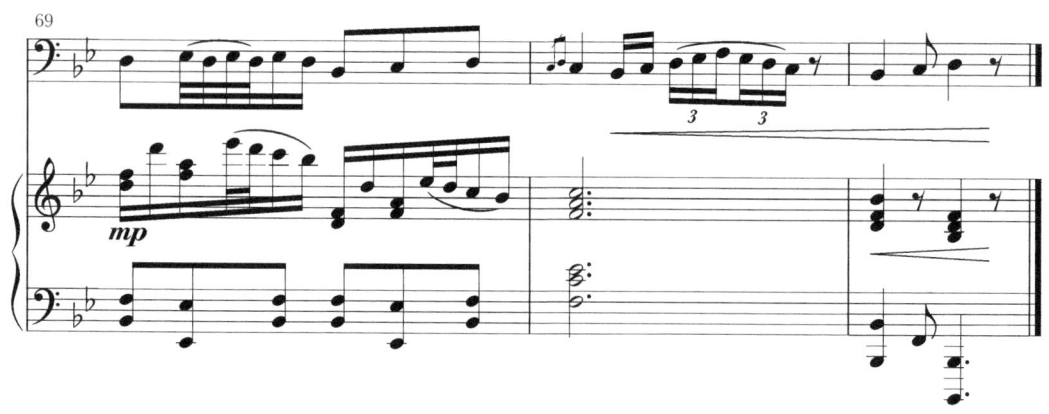

Three Plus One

'Spectroscopy' - Part Four

Jack Mitchell Smith

Krishna

'Spectroscopy' - Part Five

Jack Mitchell Smith

Whisper of the Soul

'Spectroscopy' - Part Six

Jack Mitchell Smith

Murex Shell

'Spectroscopy' - Part Seven

Jack Mitchell Smith

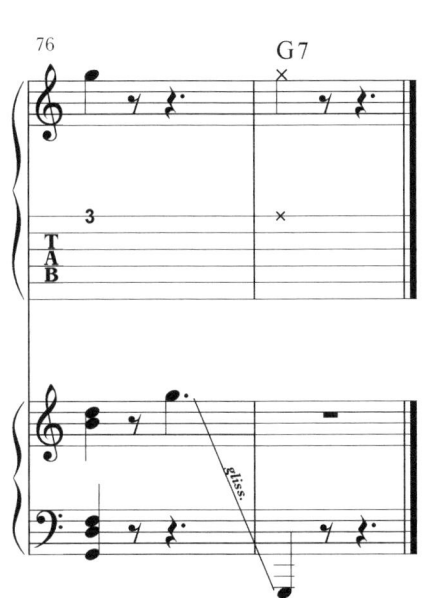